MW00680811

NINJA FOODI DIGITAL AIR FRY OVEN COOKBOOK 2021

365 Days of Affordable, Quick and Easy Ninja Air Fry Oven Recipes for Sheet Pan Meals.

belinda turner

Table of Contents

Table of Contents

Ninja Foodi

How does it work? Ninja Foodi has been tested to see if it can be used to prepare French fries, crunchy chicken, cheesecake, chicken patties, and other basic products in stand-alone pressure cookers and fryers.

Accessories Everywhere

The Foodi is selling for the 6.5-liter version between 1

90 and 230 US dollars, but the exact price depends on where you buy it. It sounds like lots of money, but you get a lot for that price.

One of the first things we noticed when Foodi arrived was that the capacity of the box is exceptionally high compared to instant pressure cookers and pressure cookers with similar cooking appliances. The fast cooking capacity of the Foodi is 6.5 liters, while the fryer can hold 4 liters.

When you open the big box, you'll find the Ninja Foodi oval hob with an air cooker lid and pressure cooker, as well as a sealing ring, a PTFE and PFOA-free ceramic tub, a cooking basket with air, an adjustable roasting pan. Side handles, condensate cup, cookbook, cooking instructions, and user guide.

Advantages Of Frying Without Oil (Air Fryer)

The traditional frying process involves introducing the food in a container with oil at high temperatures, between 150 and 200 °C. The oil transmits the heat and quickly heats the ingredient and evenly.

This time we will talk about a new way of frying oil without food. Is it possible? Of course, you will see the explanation on how to do it and the advantages of this method:

How to fry without oil?

New air fryers on the market do not require oil or maybe just a little to cook food. They work with a system that incorporates hot air and takes advantage of the natural fat that fresh or frozen Ingredients have.

To obtain more crispy results, just add a spoonful of oil. Almost nothing compared to the amount used in a cheap conventional fryer.

With this technique, in addition to low caloric content, you will have rich dishes. You enjoy this crunchy texture but without the need to resort to large amounts of oil and, therefore, fats.

Advantages You Get When Frying Without Oil (Air Fryer)

Frying without oil is a way to enjoy crispy foods without falling into the use of too much oil. The advantages of the Air fryer are the following:

• Ideal to eat healthily. Calories decrease when using an air fryer because the amount of oil used is minimal or even nil.

• Food with rich flavor, in this form of cooking, do not give off odors. There is also no risk of the flavors mixing if you have already prepared another food with a strong flavor.

• Frying without oil does not allow food to oxidize, and there is no possibility that the oil will burn and become harmful.

• Cook and fry foods without messing everything up, free of oil splashes. When finished, it is much easier to clean the surroundings and the hot air fryer.

1. **Peppers Stuffed With Potato Omelet**

Preparation Time: 30 Min
Serving: 4
Ingredients

- 2 large peppers
- 2 medium potatoes
- 1 egg
- olive oil to taste
- salt to taste

Preparation : of tortilla-filled peppers

1. Preheat the Air fryer oven without oil at 180ºC. for 4 minutes
2. Peel the potatoes and slice them into squares for easy handling
3. Place the potatoes on a plate and spray them with olive oil and a little pepper and salt
4. Place it in the fryer basket for 12 minutes and remove it halfway through cooking
5. Cut the peppers in half, remove the seeds and add salt
6. Beat those egg and then mix it with the potatoes once cooked
7. Fill the peppers with the mixture and place them in the Air fryer again for 7 minutes at 200 ° C.

As mentioned earlier this recipe is quite flexible, it can be made with green, red or yellow peppers. You can add more with red pepper since the taste is sweeter. For a more intense flavor, green peppers are recommended. The filling on this occasion is with potato omelet but it can also be made with mushrooms or vegetables. Enjoy your meal!

Nutritional Information:

- Fat: 20.11 g
- Saturated fatty acids: 11 g
- Protein / protein: 14.49 g

- Roughage: 9.02 g
- Added sugar: 0 g
- Calories: 474

2. Recipe Potato Chips without Oil

Preparation Time: 40 Min
Serving: 4
Ingredients
For 4 servings
- 2 large potatoes
- 1 tablespoon of olive oil
- Salt to taste

Preparation
1. Peel the potatoes and cut them on a regular basis
2. Preheat the Air fryer oven without oil at 180 ° C
3. Put the potatoes in the Air fryer without oil for 25 minutes
4. Add salt to taste

3. Maroni Fry in the Hot Air Fryer

Preparation Time: 30 Min
Serving: 4
<u>Ingredients</u>
25 ounce of chestnuts
<u>Preparation:</u>

1. Fry for the chestnuts in the hot air fryer oven the chestnuts in cold water for about 1 hour in fryer. Then cut with a small knife on one side thinly crosswise.
2. Distribute the chestnuts on the grill cup and bake at 170 ° C for about 25-30 minutes with occasional shaking.
3. When roasting chestnuts fry in the hot fryer during the baking process about 80 ml of water in the bottom of the Air fryer hot air fryer to prevent drying of the chestnuts.
4. Serve the chestnuts, for example, in home-made paper bags or in a homemade gift box. When roasting chestnuts in the Air fryer wait with a big cup mulled wine and then enjoy the hot chestnuts right away.

4. Baked Vegetables from the Hot Air Fryer

Preparation Time: 15-30 Min
Serving: 4
Ingredients

- 1 piece of broccoli
- 1 piece of zucchini
- 8.7 ounce mushrooms To bread:
- 150 g of flour (smooth)
- 5.2 ounce of crumbs
- 2-3 eggs
- salt
- 1 teaspoon sunflower oil

Preparation:

1. For the baked vegetables, cut the broccoli with a small knife, remove the stalk and halve the broccoli roses if necessary.
2. Boil in boiling salted water for approx. 20 seconds, then cool in ice-cold water (= blanching). Let it dry on kitchen paper.
3. Cut off the ends of the zucchini, slicing the rest diagonally into about 1 cm thick slices. Clean mushrooms, halve large mushrooms or quarter them.
4. Turn the vegetables into flour first, pull them through the whisked, salted eggs and then bread with the crumbs.
5. Add the vegetables to the Air Fryer add some oil to the oven and bake at 185 ° C for about 8-10 minutes until crisp.
6. The baked vegetable dish and serve with a dipping sauce of your choice.
7. The baked vegetables are best served with sauce remolded or tartar sauce and salad garnished. Instead of sunflower oil, rapeseed oil is also ideal for frying.

5. Blueberry pancakes from the hot air fryer

Ingredients
Preparation Time: 13 Min
Serving: 2

- 3 egg whites
- 1 tbsp sugar
- 0.5 cup of milk
- 0.2 ounce of flour
- 3 egg yolks
- 0.3 ounce of blueberries
- 0.1 ounce of almond slivers
- lemon juice
- 1 shot of rum (or Rumaroma)
- 1 tbsp vanilla sugar
- 1 pinch of salt
- 1 tsp butter
- Icing sugar (for dusting)

Preparation:

1. For the blueberry pancake in a bowl, beat the egg whites with sugar until they are solid.
2. In another bowl, add milk, flour, egg yolks, blueberries, almonds, lemon juice, rum, vanilla sugar and a pinch of salt until smooth.

3. Gently lift the egg whites under the dough. Add 1 tsp butter to the dish, pour the dough into the baking pan of the air deep fryer and bake at 180 ° C for 10-13 minutes.
4. Dust the dust with icing sugar and allow caramelizing for another 5 minutes.
5. Then remove the insert and pluck the blueberry pancake with 2 wooden spoons.
6. To match cranberries and applesauce.
7. You can do this putty all year round. Simply replace the blueberries with a fruit that is currently in season.

Nutritional Information:

- Calories 520
- Calories from Fat 126
- Total Fat 14g 22%
- Polyunsaturated Fat 2g
- Monounsaturated Fat 5.3g
- Cholesterol 58mg 19%
- Sodium 1104mg 46%
- Potassium 250.56mg 7%
- Carbohydrates 90.9g 30%
- Dietary Fiber 0g 0%
- Sugars 0g
- Protein 8.3g

6. Deep Fried Meatballs from the Hot Air Fryer

Preparation Time: 15-30 Min
Serving: 4
Ingredients
- 3.5 ounce of Ground meat (mixed)
- One piece of bread (from the previous day)
- Two pieces of onions (finely chopped)
- 1 tbsp parsley (finely chopped)
- 1 tbsp olive oil
- Salt
- 3 tbsp breadcrumbs
- Pepper

Preparation
1. For the fried meatballs, soak the Semmelin water and squeeze out. Knead minced, crushed rolls, chopped onions, parsley and olive oil to a smooth mass season with salt and pepper.
2. Form some small balls and roll each of them in the bread crumbs. Put the meatballs into the basket of the hot air fryer oven and bake in 20 minutes at 200 ° C (without adding fat).
3. Serve the fried meatballs while still hot.

Tip
The fried meatballs served with a dipping sauce of your choice.

Preparation Time: 30 Min
Serving: 4
Ingredients

- 3.4 ounce of white potatoes
- 2 tablespoons of olive oil
- 1 tablespoon of spicy paprika
- Freshly ground black pepper
- 0.6 ounce of Greek yogurt

Preparation

1. Preheat the air fryer oven to 180 degrees. Peel the potatoes and then slice it into cubes of 3 cm. Dip the cubes in water for at least 30 minutes. Dry them well with paper towels.
2. In a medium-sized bowl, mix 1 tablespoon of olive oil with the paprika and add pepper to taste. Cover the potato cubes with the spiced oil.
3. Place the potato cubes in the fryer basket and insert it into the air fryer. Set the timer to 20 minutes and fry the dice until they are golden and ready to drink. Give them turns once in a while.
4. In a small bowl, mix the Greek yogurt with the remaining spoonful of olive oil and add salt and pepper to taste. Spread the paprika over the mixture. Serve the yogurt as a sauce with the potatoes.
5. Serve the potato cubes on a tray and salt them.

8. Beef Roulades

Preparation Time: 60 Min
Serving: 4
Ingredients

- Four beef schnitzel
- Salt
- Pepper
- Mustard
- Tomato paste
- Four slices of bacon (lean)
- One onion (cut into rings)
- Pickle
- 1 cup of rice (cooked)

For the sauce:

- Roots
- One onion (medium)
- 1 Stamper apricot brandy

Preparation

1. For the beef roulades, beat the schnitzel, salt, pepper, and coat on one side with tomato paste and mustard. Place the bacon slices on top and spread onion rings, cucumber strips and rice.
2. Roll up the schnitzel, fix with a toothpick and fry in Air fryer oven.
3. Take out the beef roulades. Roast the chopped onion and the noodled root system thoroughly in the roasting stock, pour water over it and gently soften the roulades.

4. Before serving, pass the vegetables with the juice to a sauce. Cook well and deglaze with apricot brandy. Just season if necessary.
5. Pour the sauce over the beef roulades and serve them hot.
6. To beef roulades also match potatoes.

Nutritional Information

- Saturated Fat 6.4g grams
- Trans Fat 0.7g grams
- 41%Cholesterol 123mg milligrams
- 35%Sodium 844mg milligrams
- 15%Potassium 538mg milligrams
- 5%Total Carbohydrates 14g grams
- 5% Dietary Fiber 1.2g grams
- Sugars 6.1g grams

9. **Asparagus vegetables from the Air fryer**

Preparation Time: 15-30 Min
Serving: 2
Ingredients

- 4 bars of asparagus (white)
- 4 bars of asparagus (green)
- 1 tbsp butter
- One pinch of salt
- Pepper
- Sugar
- Two pcs. Paradeiser (gutted, diced)

- 1 ounce of soup
- Two sprigs of lemon balm (leaves peeled, chopped)

Preparation

1. For the asparagus Wash the asparagus, peel, remove ends, cut into small pieces and mix with the butter, one pinch of salt, pepper, and sugar.
2. Core the Paradeiser and cut into fine cubes.
3. Add the asparagus to the baking tray add the soup and heat at 160 ° C in the Philips Air fryer Hot Air Fryer oven.
4. After about 12-15 minutes add the dice and cook for another 5 minutes.
5. Then remove the asparagus and stir chopped lemon balm under the finished asparagus.

Nutritional Information

- Total Fat 0.1 g   0%
- Total Carbohydrate 3.9 g   1%
- Dietary fiber 2.1 g   8%
- Sugar 1.9 g
- Protein 2.2 g   4%

Grenadier Pancakes with Fried Egg from the Hot Air Fryer

Preparation Time: 30-60 Min
Serving: 2
<u>Ingredients</u>
- 0.8 ounce of potatoes (cooked the day before)
- 0.6 of ounce noodles (cooked, or, if available, dumpling leftovers)
- 250 g leek
- 1.8 ounce of bacon
- 0.2 ounce of cured meat
- 1/2 piece of onion (white, peeled)
- 1-2 toes of garlic (peeled)
- 0.1 ounce of butter
- Two eggs
- ½ tsp. of marjoram (dried)
- ½ tsp caraway (ground)
- Salt
- Pepper (from the mill)
- 1/2 bunch chives

<u>Preparation</u>
1. For Grenadier schmarrn with fried egg bacon and cut into strips or cubes. Dice the onion and garlic, wash the leek, dry and cut into fine rings.
2. Cut the potatoes into 2 x 2 cm cubes and fry them with some butter in the baking pan of the Air fryer hot air fryer oven for 7 minutes at 180 ° C. Add the remaining ingredients, except the eggs, to the potatoes and mix well.

3. Finish stirring for an additional 20 minutes at 170 ° C with occasional stirring. Fry the fried eggs and serve the grenadier pancakes garnished with fried eggs and freshly cut chives.

Tip: Grenadier pancakes with a fried egg are a great leftover and can be varied or supplemented with other ingredients.

11. Zucchini sticks in oil-free fryer / oven

Preparation Time: 20 Min
Serving: 3
Ingredients

- 16 pcs of canes
- 1 zucchini
- Two eggs
- 1 cup of flour
- 1 lemon
- 1 cup of grated cheese and breadcrumbs

Preparation

1. Cut into sticks (or slices if desired) the zucchini (taking out its tips but with a shell!)
2. Have a bowl with flour, another with peppered eggs and a last one with lemon zest, grated cheese and breadcrumbs all together and mixed
3. Pass all the zucchinis for flour, then for the eggs and finally for the mixture of lemon, cheese and breadcrumbs.
4. Take a fryer without oil or preheated oven for approx. 20 min. And ready!!! Delis are warm and with soy sauce or ketchup

12. Pumpkin croquettes using oil-free fryer

Preparation Time: 20 Min
Serving: 3
Ingredient s

- Pumpkin puree
- 1 onion
- 1 tbsp. or 2 tbsps. grated cheese
- Eggs
- Bread crumbs
- Port health light cheese

Preparation

1. Make pumpkin puree. (Half a pumpkin left in the oven
2. Sauté chopped onion, cooked it in water and they are very good.
3. Mix in a bowl, pumpkin, grated cheese, onion, salt, pepper and nutmeg.
4. Assemble the croquettes, and put cheese, use port health light, in the middle, go through breadcrumbs, beaten egg and breadcrumbs.
5. Use a fryer oven without oil, so put vegetable spray, 200 degrees and 20 minutes, and they are full.

13.   Vegetables in Airfryer

Preparation Time: 35 Mins
Serving: 2
Ingredients

- 2 potatoes
- 1 zucchini
- 1 onion
- 1 red pepper
- 1 green pepper

Preparation

1. We cut the potatoes into slices.
2. We cut the onion into rings
3. We cut the zucchini slices
4. We cut the peppers into strips.
5. We put the entire bowl and add a little salt, ground pepper and some extra virgin olive oil.
6. We mix well.
7. We pass to the basket of the Airfryer oven.
8. We select 160 degrees, 30 minutes.
9. We check that the vegetables are to our liking; put the last 5 minutes at 180 degrees to brown more.
10. We serve

14. Air-Fried Breakfast Bombs

Preparation Time: 10 Mins
Serving: 2
Ingredients

- 3 center-cut bacon slices
- 3 giant eggs, gently crushed
- 1-ounce 1/3-less-fat cheese, softened
- 1 tablespoon shredded contemporary chives
- 4 ounces contemporary ready cereal pizza pie dough
- Cooking spray

Preparation

1. Cook bacon is in a medium cooking pan over medium till very crisp, concerning ten minutes. Take away bacon from the pan; crumble. Add eggs to the bacon drippings in pan; cook, stirring usually, till nearly set however still loose, concerning one minute. Transfer eggs to a bowl; stir in cheese, chives, and broken bacon.
2. Divide dough into four equal items. Roll each bit on a gently floured surface into a 5-inch circle. Place quarter of egg mixture in center of every dough circle. Brush outside fringe of dough with water; wrap dough around egg mixture to make a handbag, pinching along dough at the seams.
3. Put dough purses in single layer in air fryer oven ; coat well with change of state spray. Cook at 350°F till golden brown, five to six minutes, checking once four minutes.

Nutritional info

- Calories 305
- Fat 15g
- Satfat 5g
- Unsatfat 8g
- Protein 19g
- Carbohydrate 26g

- Fiber 2g
- Sugars 1g
- Added sugars 0g
- Sodium 548mg
- Calcium 105 DV
- Potassium 2 DV

15.   Chicken Wings and French Fries

Preparation Time: 40 Mins
Serving: 4
Ingredients:

- 0.50 ounce of clean chicken wings
- A teaspoon of garlic powder
- Salt
- Pepper
- A teaspoon of olive oil
- 2 medium potatoes

Preparation

1. We heat the fryer oven without air at 180 ºc for 5 minutes.
2. Meanwhile, pepper the chicken and add a teaspoon of olive oil, mix everything well and put in the fryer basket.
3. It is essential not to put too much to do well.
4. We leave 20 minutes in total, but after 10 minutes we have to turn the meat to make it on both sides.
5. If you like much more golden leave more time and go.
6. While the wings are done we peel, wash and cut the potatoes; We will also add a pinch of salt.
7. When we have the chicken, we preheat again to 200ºC and put the previously drained potatoes since they will have released some water.
8. We will have 16 minutes at 8 to move them so that they are done equally.
9. You will see how good the result is fantastic.

Air-Fried Hot Chicken Thighs

Preparation Time: 15-25 Min
Serving: 2
Ingredients

- 2 cups low-fat milk
- 1 teaspoon paprika
- 1/2 teaspoon cayenne pepper
- 4 (6- to 7-oz.) boneless, skinless chicken thighs
- 1 cup (about four 1/4 oz.) general flour
- 2 giant eggs
- 2 tablespoons water
- 2 cups cereal panko (Japanese-style breadcrumbs)
- 1/2 teaspoon kosher salt
- Cooking spray
- 2 teaspoons sauce (such as Franks RedHot)

Preparation

1. Combine milk, paprika, and cayenne pepper in an exceedingly giant bowl. Add chicken thighs, and switch to coat. Cowl and infuse in white goods a minimum of half dozen hours or long.
2. Place flour in an exceedingly shallow dish. Gently whisk along eggs and water in an exceedingly second shallow dish. Place panko in an exceedingly third shallow dish. Take away chicken from marinade; discard marinade. Sprinkle chicken with salt. Dredge in flour, shaking off excess. Dip in egg mixture, permitting excess to drip off. Dredge in panko, pressing to stick. Coat chicken on either side with change of state spray.
3. Lightly spray air fryer basket with change of state spray. Place chicken in single layer within the basket, and cook in batches at 400°F till a measuring device inserted in chicken registers 165°F and coating is golden brown and tender, 16 minutes, turning chicken over halfway through change of state.

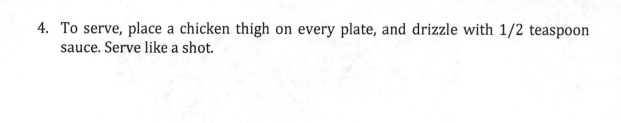

4. To serve, place a chicken thigh on every plate, and drizzle with 1/2 teaspoon sauce. Serve like a shot.

17. Air fryer Baked Stuffed Fish

Preparation Time: 30 Mins
Serving: 2
Ingredients
- 1 tiny fillet of fish
- 0.06 ounce of brown breadcrumbs (½ slice of brown bread)
- 1 tiny low onion, chopped
- 1 teaspoon finely chopped parsley (or 1 teaspoon dried parsley) or a pinch of mixed herbs
- ½ teaspoon of oil
- A touch juices

Preparation
1. Pre-heat the kitchen air fryer oven to 180°C or 350°F or Gas Mark four.
2. Clean and prepare fish. Dry in room paper.
3. Combine breadcrumbs, sliced onion, and parsley or mixed
4. Herbs, salt and pepper in a very tiny bowl.
5. Heat oil and stir into crumb mixture. Finally
6. Add a touch skin or juice.
7. Bake for 20–30 minutes, betting on size and thickness of fish.
8. Elevate fish fastidiously on to a warm dish and surround with seared peas, lemon wedges and parsley.
9. 2 adults

18.   Air fryer Tuna fast bake

Preparation Time: 25 Mins
Serving: 3
Ingredients

- A pair of cans of tuna in brine or drained (198g or 7oz)
- 1 onion, chopped
- Parsley sauce
- 1 teaspoon Worcester sauce
- Pinch of salt if desired
- Pepper
- Knob of low-fat unfold
- 8 oz or 225g contemporary brown breadcrumbs (6 slices)

Preparation

1. Flake the tuna and blend along with the onion, white parsley, sauce, Worchester sauce, salt and pepper
2. Pour a number of the fish sauce into a casserole dish. Add a layer of breadcrumbs, followed by a layer of sauce
3. Continue layering during this method till all the ingredients are used up.
4. End with a layer of breadcrumbs on the highest, dot the surface
5. With the low-fat unfold and bake within the pre-heated kitchen air fryer for 20–25 minutes.
6. Serve right away

Serve with spud or dish

Preparation Time: 60 Mins
Serving: 2
<u>**Ingredients**</u>
- 8 chicken thighs or legs
- a pair of medium onions thinly sliced
- Pinch of salt if desired
- Pepper
- 1 sweet pepper thinly sliced
- 5 dessert spoons spaghetti sauce
- 1 containerful Worcester sauce
- 1 teaspoon chili powder

<u>**Preparation**</u>
1. Pre-heat the kitchen air fryer oven to 190°C or 375°F or Gas Mark five.
2. Combine all ingredients except the chicken to create the sauce.
3. Organize the chicken during a single layer within the casserole dish.
4. Spoon sauce over the chicken.
5. Cowl and bake for 55–60 minutes, till the chicken is tender.

Preparation Time: 14 Mins
Serving: 2
Ingredients
- 4 ears recent corn (about 1 1/2 avoirdupois Unit.), shucked
- Cooking spray
- 1, 1/2 tablespoons unseasoned butter
- 2 teaspoons cut garlic
- one teaspoon lime zest and 1 Tbsp. recent juice (from 1 lime)
- 1/2 teaspoon kosher salt
- 1/2 teaspoon black pepper
- 2 tablespoons cut recent cilantro

Preparation
1. Lightly coat corn is with preparation spray, and place in a very single layer in air fryer oven . Cook at 400°F till tender and slightly burn, 14 minutes, turning corn over halfway through preparation.
2. Meanwhile, stir along butter, garlic, lime zest, and juice in a very tiny microwavable bowl. Air fryer on HIGH till butter is dissolved and garlic is sweet-smelling, regarding thirty seconds. Place corn on a platter then pour over butter mixture. Sprinkle with salt, pepper, and cilantro. Serve instantly.

Nutritional info
- Calories 201
- Fat 7g
- Sat fat 3g
- Unsatfat 3g
- Protein 6

- Carbohydrate 35g
- Fiber 4g
- Sugars 12
- Added sugars 0
- Sodium 269m
- Calcium 1 Chronicles DV
- Potassium 11 DV

21. Air-Fried Sweet Potato Fries

Preparation Time: 14 Mins
Serving: 2

Ingredients

- 1 tablespoon oil
- 1 teaspoon cut recent thyme
- 1/4 teaspoon fine ocean salt
- 1/4 teaspoon garlic powder
- 2 (6-oz.) sweet potatoes, bare-assed and dig 1/4-inch sticks
- Cooking spray

Preparation

1. Stir along oil, thyme, salt, and garlic powder in a very medium size bowl. Add sweet potato, toss well to coat.
2. Lightly coat air fryer oven is with preparation spray. Place sweet potatoes in single layer within the basket, and cook in batches at 400°F till tender on the within and gently brunet on the skin, 14 minutes, turning fries over halfway through preparation.

Nutritional info

- Calories 104
- Fat 3g
- Protein 1g
- Carbohydrate 17g
- Fiber 3g
- Sugars 4g

Preparation Time: 10 Mins
Serving: 2
Ingredients

- 4 (6-in.) up whole-grain flour tortillas
- 4 ounces reduced-fat sharp store cheese, cut (about one cup)
- 1 cup of sliced red bell pepper
- 1 cup of sliced zucchini
- 1 cup of no-salt-added canned black beans, drained and rinsed
- Cooking spray
- 2 ounces plain two reduced-fat Greek food
- one teaspoon lime zest and 1 Tbsp. contemporary juice (from one lime)
- 1/4 teaspoon ground cumin
- 2 tablespoons shredded contemporary cilantro
- 1/2 cup drained cold pico DE gallo

Preparations

1. Place tortillas on a piece surface. Sprinkle two tablespoons cut cheese over half every flannel-cake. High cheese on every flannel-cake with 1/4 cup every red pepper slice, zucchini slices, and black beans. Sprinkle equally with remaining 1/2 cup cheese. Fold tortillas over to make half-moon formed quesadillas. Gently coat quesadillas with change of state spray, and secure with toothpicks.

2. Lightly spray air fryer oven with change of state spray. Fastidiously place two quesadillas within the basket, and cook at 400°F till tortillas golden brown and slightly tender, cheese is liquified, and vegetables slightly softened, 10 minutes, turning quesadillas over halfway through change of state. Repeat with remaining quesadillas.

3. While quesadillas cook, stir along food, lime zest, lime juice, and cumin in an exceedingly tiny bowl. To serve, cut every quesadilla into wedges and sprinkle with cilantro. Serve every with one tablespoon cumin cream and a couple of tablespoons pico DE gallo.

23. Loaded Greek Feta Fries

Preparation Time: 30 Mins
Serving: 3

Ingredients

- Cooking spray
- 2 (7-oz.) Yukon Gold or russet potatoes clean and dried
- 1 tablespoon oil
- 2 teaspoons of lemon rind
- 1/2 teaspoon of dried oregano
- 1/4 teaspoon of kosher salt
- 1/4 teaspoon of garlic powder
- 1/4 teaspoon of onion powder
- 1/4 teaspoon of paprika
- 1/4 teaspoon of black pepper
- 2 ounces feta cheese, finely grated (about 1/2 cup)
- 2 ounces cut skinless rotisserie pigeon breast
- 1/4 cup of ready tzatziki
- 1/4 cup of seeded and diced plum tomato
- 2 tablespoons of shredded Spanish onion
- 1 tablespoon of shredded contemporary Italian parsley and oregano

Preparations

1. Preheat AN air fryer oven to 380°F. Coat the basket with change of state spray.
2. Cut every potato lengthwise into 1/4-inch-thick slices; cut every go 1/4-inch fry.
3. Toss along the potatoes and oil in an exceedingly giant bowl. Season with zest, dried oregano, salt, garlic powder, onion powder, paprika, and pepper; toss to coat.
4. In two batches, cook the seasoned potatoes till crisp, concerning quarter-hour, flipping fries halfway through change of state time.
5. Return the primary batch of fries to the basket, and cook till warm through, one to two minutes. Take away from air fryer. High fries with half the feta, chicken, tzatziki, remaining feta, tomato, red onion, and contemporary herbs.

Nutritional info

- Calories 383
- Fat 16g
- Satfat 7g
- Unsatfat 8g
- Protein 19g
- Carbohydrate 42g
- Fiber 4g
- Sugars 5g
- Added sugars 0g
- Sodium 654mg

- Calcium 21 DV
- Potassium 29 DV

24.   Pork head chops with vegetables in Airfryer

Preparation Time: 15 Mins
Serving: 2-4
Ingredients

- 4 pork head chops
- 2 red tomatoes
- 1 large green pepper
- 4 mushrooms
- 1 onion
- 4 slices of cheese
- Salt
- Ground pepper
- Extra virgin olive oil

Preparations

1. We put the four chops on a plate and salt and pepper.
2. We put two of the chops in the Airfryer oven.
3. Place tomato slices, cheese slices, pepper slices, onion slices and mushroom slices.
4. We add some threads of oil.
5. We take the Airfryer and select 180 degrees, 15 minutes.
6. We check that the meat is well made and we take out.
7. We repeat the same method with the other two pork chops.
8. We serve

Nutritional info

- Calories 383
- Protein 19g
- Carbohydrate 42g

25.   Grilled Chicken Spice Ribs, Airfryer Recipe

Preparation Time: 40 Mins
Serving: 2
Ingredients

- 2.1 ounce of ribs
- Roasted Chicken Seasoning
- Extra virgin olive oil

Preparation

1. We put the ribs in a bowl and add some strands of extra virgin olive oil.
2. We stir well so that the oil permeates the ribs well.
3. Season with roasted chicken seasoning, the amount we want. If it is the first time you use it, put just enough to impregnate the ribs and once you try it, you decide if you put more or less for future recipes. Put enough, permeate the ribs well because the seasoning gives flavor but is not spicy.
4. We stir well so that the seasoning mixes well with all the ribs.

5. We place the ribs in the oven of the Airfryer.
6. We select 180 degrees, 40 minutes.
7. From time to time we remove the ribs so that they are browned on all their faces.
8. Once the program ends, we check that the ribs are to our liking. We can always select more time if, we see that they are not fully made because the ribs are very thick, or because we like them more golden.
9. We serve

Chicken with thyme in Airfryer

Preparation Time: 40 Mins

Serving: 4

Ingredients

- 1 chicken
- 8 cloves of garlic
- 1 lemon
- Thyme
- Salt
- Ground pepper
- Extra virgin olive oil

Preparation

1. Chop the chicken into small pieces. We remove or not remove the skin, to everyone's taste.
2. We put in a large bowl all the chicken and salt and pepper.
3. Peel the garlic, hit each clove of garlic and add it to the chicken.
4. Squeeze the lemon and then add the juice to the chicken.
5. Sprinkle with thyme.
6. We stir the entire chicken well so that all the ingredients are linked.
7. Cover with paper films and take to the refrigerator, minimum 2 hours.
8. We passed the chicken to the basket of the Airfryer.
9. Add a few strands of extra virgin olive oil and stir.
10. We take the Airfryer and select 40 minutes, 170 degrees.
11. We serve

NOTE. If we do not fit all the chicken, we will have to do in two batches.

Preparation Time: 20 Mins

Serving: 4

Ingredients

- 1 bag of ham croquettes
- 1 bag of mixed salad
- 1 handful of nuts
- Salad Yogurt Sauce
- Salt

Preparation

1. We wash the lettuce and drain well.
2. We put the croquettes in the oven of the Airfryer and paint with a little oil.
3. We select 20 minutes, 180 degrees.
4. We spread the salad between four dishes.
5. We distribute the croquettes between the four dishes.
6. We add a stream of yogurt sauce in each salad.
7. We decorate with peeled walnuts.
8. We serve

28.   Chicken Tears

Preparation Time: 20 Mins
Serving: 4
Ingredients

- 2 chicken breasts
- Flour
- Salt
- Ground pepper
- Extra virgin olive oil
- Lemon juice
- Garlic powder

Preparations

1. Cut the chicken breasts into tears. We season and put some lemon juice and garlic powder. Let's flirt well.
2. We go through flour and shake.
3. Place the tears in the oven of the Airfryer and paint with extra virgin olive oil.
4. We select 180 degrees, 20 minutes.
5. We move from time to time so that the tears are made on all their faces.
6. We serve

Preparation Time: 14 Mins

Serving: 4

Ingredients

- 1.3 ounce chicken breast
- 0.4 ounce of cream cheese
- 1 egg
- Bread crumbs
- Salt
- Ground pepper

Preparation

1. We put the chicken breast in the Cuisine with the blades ultrablade.
2. We pepper and select speed 12, 30 seconds.
3. Add the cheese and put speed 12, 30 seconds.
4. We take out the dough and make the nuggets.
5. We go through beaten egg and breadcrumbs.
6. We put in the oven of the Airfryer.
7. We select 5 minutes, 180 degrees.
8. We check that they are golden to taste.
9. We put more time or serve.
10.   Do not pile up the nuggets; it is preferable to do in several batches that stick to each other.

30. Air fryer Spicy Meatballs

Serve with vegetables and alimentary paste, rice or potatoes

Preparation Time: 20 Mins

Serving: 2

Ingredients

- 1.9 ounce lean minced beef
- 1 giant onion finely cut
- Two–3 cloves of garlic finely cut
- 1 teaspoon ginger (optional)
- 2 dessert spoonful's flavored
- 1 dessertspoon starch or flour

Preparation

1. Place the minced meat in a very giant bowl.
2. Fry the onion and garlic till golden brown.
3. Combine the flavored, ginger and starch or flour with a
4. Little water and boost air fryer oven . Cook for some minutes.
5. Add this mixture to the mincemeat and blend well.
6. Form meatballs with damp hands.
7. Drain excess fat from the pan or gently pat meatballs with
8. Kitchen paper to get rid of any excess fat
9. Fry gently for 15–20 minutes, turning often

31. Air fryer Beef Loaf receipt

Serve with vegetables or cold with a dish or a sandwich filling

Preparation Time: 3 hours

Serving: 2

Ingredients

- 1.9 ounce lean minced beef
- 1 massive onion, terribly finely sliced
- 4oz contemporary brown readcrumbs (4 slices)
- Pinch of salt if desired
- Pepper
- 2 dessertspoons spaghetti sauce
- 2.5 ounce of home-brewed chicken or vegetable
- Stock or 1 low-salt stock
- Dissolved inside 2.5 ounce of boiling water
- 1 egg, beaten

Preparation

1. Place all the ingredients during a massive bowl and blend totally along.
2. Brush an outsized loaf tin with oil and fill with the mixture.
3. Swish the highest with a spatula and place within the electric refrigerator for 1 hour.
4. Pre-heat the kitchen air fryer oven to 180°C or 350°F or Gas Mark four.
5. Cook within the pre-heated kitchen air fryer for 1¼–1½ hours.

Preparation Time: 25 Mins
Serving: 2

Ingredients

- 4 beef steaks
- Slices of cured ham
- Roasted peppers
- To breach flour, egg and breadcrumbs
- Extra virgin olive oil
- Salt
- Ground pepper

Preparation

1. We season the fillets and fill with slices of cured ham and roasted red peppers.
2. We press well and pass through flour, beaten egg and breadcrumbs to breach them well.
3. We paint everything very well with extra virgin olive oil. Keep it wet.
4. We place in the oven of the Airfryer and select 15 minutes at 160 degrees and 10 minutes more at 180 degrees.
5. When we see that they are well browned on the outside, we take out.
6. If we have to leave more time, we select another 10 minutes at 180 degrees.
7. Remember that it has to be very well painted with oil so that they are a beautiful golden color.

33.   Serve with stewed rice or potatoes

Preparation Time: 1hr; 30 Mins
Serving: 2
Ingredients

- 1½ avoirdupois unit or 2.9 ounce stewing beef
- 1 dessertspoonful oil
- 3 onions, in the buff and sliced
- Pinch of salt if desired
- Pepper
- Tin of cut tomatoes
- ½ dessertspoonful paprika
- 1 dessertspoonful tomato puree
- 1 atomic number 78 or 2.5 ounce water
- 6–8 potatoes, in the buff and sliced
- 1 clove garlic crushed

Preparation

1. Take away the fat from the meat and take away one-inch cubes.
2. Heat the oil in an air fryer. Add the cubes of beef some at a time and fry them till they're brown on all sides.
3. Transfer the brunet meat to a pan.
4. Fry the onions within the air fryer till they're golden brown.
5. Stir within the tomatoes, garlic, paprika, tomato puree, salt and pepper.
6. Add this to the brunet meat. Then add the water. Arouse boil, stirring all time
7. Cowl with a lid and cook slowly for 1 hour.
8. Add the sliced potatoes and simmer for an additional half-hour approximately.

34.   Budin meat

Preparation Time: 35 Mins
Serving: 4
Ingredients

- 1.7 ounce lean minced beef
- 1 lightly beaten egg
- 3 tablespoons breadcrumbs
- 50 g of salami or chorizo well chopped
- 1 small onion, well chopped
- 1 tablespoon fresh thyme
- Freshly ground pepper
- 2 mushrooms in thick slices
- 1 tablespoon olive oil

Preparation

1. Preheat the airfryer oven to 200 ° C.
2. Mix minced meat inside a bowl with the egg, breadcrumbs, salami, onion, thyme, 1 teaspoon of salt and a generous amount of pepper. Knead it all right.

3. Pass the minced meat to the tray or platter and smooth the top. Place the mushrooms by pressing a little and cover the top with olive oil.
4. Place the tray or dish in the basket and insert it into the airfryer. Set the timer to 25 minutes and roast the meat pudding until it has a nice toasted color and is well done.
5. Let the pudding stand at least 10 minutes before serving. Then cut it into wedges. It is delicious with chips and salad.

35. Air fryer Lamb scallop Casserole

Preparation Time: 13 Mins

Serving: 3

Pork chops may even be used

Ingredients

- 1 dessert spoonful of oil
- 8 lamb cutlets
- 2 giant onions, in the buff and sliced thickly into rings
- 5 potatoes, in the buff and thinly sliced
- ½ atomic number 78 or 275ml of homespun vegetable stock
- Or 1 low-salt vegetable stock
- Dissolved in ½ atomic number 78 or 275ml of boiling water
- 1 dessertspoonful flour
- 2 dessertspoons Worcestershire
- 1 teaspoon dried mixed herbs (optional)
- Pinch of salt if desired
- Pepper
- 2 carrots, chopped
- 1 parsnip, chopped

Preparations

1. Pre-heat the kitchen air fryer oven to 160°C or 325°F or Gas Mark three.
2. Part cook the potatoes in boiling salt-cured water for five minutes, then slice thinly.
3. Cook cutlets in a very cooking air fryer over an occasional heat for 5–10 minutes till brunet, turning once. Placed on a heat plate
4. Add the onions to the air fryer and cook gently for 2–3 minutes till brunet.
5. Drain off most 1 tablespoon of juice from the pan.
6. Scatter the flour within the air fryer and cook for one-minute stirring perpetually.
7. Add the stock, Worcestershire and mixed herbs. Cook till thickened.
8. Add the salt and pepper to style.
9. To assemble: gently grease a casserole dish Lay 0.5 the potatoes on the bottom, then top with lamb cutlets, carrots and parsnips. Pour over the thickened stock and onions. Lay the remainder of the potatoes on high.
10. Cook within the kitchen air fryer for forty-five minutes till cutlets area unit tender and therefore the potatoes on the surface area unit golden.

Air-Fried Pork Dumplings with Dipping Sauce

Preparation Time: 15 Mins
Serving: 2
Ingredients

- 1 teaspoon oil
- 4 cups shredded Bok choy (about 20 oz.)
- 1 tablespoon of shredded contemporary ginger
- 1 tablespoon of shredded garlic (3 garlic cloves)
- 4 ounces of ground pork
- 1/4 teaspoon crushed red pepper
- 18 (3 1/2-inch-square) of dumpling wrappers or wonton wrappers
- Cooking spray
- 2 tablespoons rice vinegar
- 2 teaspoons lower-sodium condiment
- 1 teaspoon cooked vegetable oil
- 1/2 teaspoon packed brown sugar
- 1 tablespoon finely shredded scallions

Preparations

1. Heat oil is in an exceedingly giant slippery cooking pan over medium-high. Add bok choy, and cook, stirring usually, till limp and largely dry, half dozen to eight minutes. Add ginger and garlic; cook, stirring perpetually, 1 minute. Transfer the bok choy mixture to a plate to chill five minutes. Pat the mixture dries with a towel.
2. Stir along ground pork, bok choy mixture, and crushed red pepper in an exceedingly medium bowl.
3. Place a dumpling wrapper on surface, and spoon concerning one tablespoon filling in center of wrapper. Employing a pastry brush or your fingers, gently moisten the sides of the wrapper with water. Fold wrapper over to form a half-moon form, pressing edges to seal. Repeat method with remaining wrappers and filling.
4. Lightly coat air fryer basket is with change of state spray. Place half dozen dumplings in basket, going space between each; gently spray the dumplings with change of state spray. Cook at 375°F till gently brunet, 12 minutes, turning dumplings over halfway through change of state. Repeat with remaining dumplings, keeping roast dumplings heat.
5. Meanwhile, stir along rice vinegar, soy sauce, sesame oil, sugar, and scallions in an exceedingly tiny bowl till sugar is dissolved. To serve, place three dumplings on every plate with two teaspoons sauce.

Preparation Time: 14 Mins
Serving: 2
Ingredient s

- Big potatoes
- 4 steaks Iberian prey
- 1 tbsps. olive oil
- 1 pinch paprika
- Salt

Preparation

35 minutes

1. Peel the potatoes, wash and cut for frying.
2. Put in the basket of the fryer with half a tablespoon of oil, salt and paprika, program 200º 15 minutes stirring halfway through cooking.
3. When finished remove and keep warm.
4. We put the seasoned fillets in the basket and brush with the rest of the oil, we program 200º 10 minutes.
5. We serve a super light, healthy and delicious dinner with the potatoes.

Philo pasta rolls stuffed with tuna and cheese

Preparation Time: 14 Mins

Serving: 2

Ingredients

- Films of philo pasta, as many as rolls we want to make
- Stuffed with tuna like we do for dumplings
- Grated cheese
- 1 beaten egg

Preparation

1. We prepare the tuna stuffing, I have already told you that I had the one that I had used to make some dumplings, but a stuffing of these characteristics is very easy to make. We just need a stir-fry, either onion or onion and pepper. We add the well-drained tuna and bind with tomato sauce.
2. We spread the philo pasta sheets and distribute the filling.
3. We cover grated cheese.
4. We close the rolls as if it were a spring roll, that is, first we turn from the bottom up of the philo paste to the filling, then we fold the sides towards the center and we have finished rolling.
5. We paint with beaten egg and place in the basket of the Airfryer.
6. We select 180 degrees about 10 minutes or so.
7. We serve

Preparation Time: 14 Mins
Serving: 2
Ingredients
- 1 package of wafer wafers
- Slices of bacon
- Slices of cheddar cheese
- Extra virgin olive oil

Preparation

1. We extend the wafers of empanadillas by all the table of work.

2. Chop the bacon and cheese.

3. We put a little bacon and cheese in each wafer, taking care that it stays inside the dough and not over it comes out.

4. Liamos wafers making a roll.

5. We are a turn in the tips, like candy paper.

6. Place in the basket of the Airfryer and paint with a brush and extra virgin olive oil.

7. We select 10 minutes, 180 degrees.

8. We will repeat until all the bacon and cheddar candies are made.

9. We serve

40.   Hake in airfryer with red pepper stir fry

Preparation Time: 20 Mins
Serving: 4
Ingredients

- 8 breaded or breaded hake fillets
- 1 large roasted red pepper
- 1 onion
- 2 carrots
- Extra virgin olive oil
- Salt
- Ground pepper
- Half a glass of wine to cook

Preparation

1. We put the hake fillets in the Airfryer, painted with extra virgin olive oil and take the Airfryer, 170 degrees, 20 minutes. We will have to do the hake in batches.
2. Meanwhile, in a large skillet we put a bottom of extra virgin olive oil and add the sliced carrots.
3. Cut the onion in julienne and add it.
4. We cut the red pepper into strips and add it too.
5. We make the sauce over medium heat until the onion is transparent.
6. We incorporate the wine and boil hard to evaporate the alcohol.
7. Add a little water and let it cook so that the carrot is finished tender. We let the liquid evaporate completely.
8. We serve the hake with the fried vegetables over the top.

41.   Fried Chicken Rear Quarters in Airfryer

Preparation Time: 14 Mins
Serving: 4
Ingredients

- 4 chicken hindquarters
- Salt
- Ground pepper
- 1 lemon
- Garlic powder
- Dried thyme
- Extra virgin olive oil
- Bread crumbs.

Preparation

1. We chop the hindquarters into small pieces.
2. We put in a bowl and salt and pepper.
3. Add the lemon juice and a few strands of extra virgin olive oil.
4. Sprinkle garlic powder and dried thyme.
5. Stir well and leave 30 minutes.

6. We go through breadcrumbs and place in the basket of the Airfryer in batches.
7. We select 180 degrees, 40 minutes.
8. We serve

Preparation Time: 15 Mins
Serving: 4
Ingredients
- 2.1 ounce of anchovies
- Salt
- Flour
- Oil spray

Preparation
1. We clean the anchovies. We can, if we want, open in half and remove the central spine.
2. We wash well, drain and put salt.
3. We pass the anchovies for flour and we place them in a large tray so that they are separated between them.
4. We spray with the oil canister so that the oil is well distributed by all of them.
5. We turn around and spray again with the oil.
6. We place the anchovies in the basket of the Airfryer so that they are not on top of each other.
7. We select 180 degrees, 15 minutes.
8. We are doing the same for a batch until we have all the fried anchovies.
9. We serve

43.   Sausage rolls in Airfryer

Preparation Time: 30 Mins

Serving: 2

Ingredients

- 24 turkey sausages
- 24 slices of turkey breast
- 24 slices of cheese
- For breading, eggs and breadcrumbs
- Extra virgin olive oil

Preparation

1. Beat the eggs in a bowl.
2. We put the breadcrumbs in another bowl.
3. We put a sausage in a slice of cheese and then in a slice of turkey breast. When we have all the sausages bundled, we proceed to breach.
4. We go through beaten egg, breadcrumbs, again beaten egg and again breadcrumbs.
5. When we have all the breaded sausages, we place 4 in the basket of the Airfryer. We paint with a little oil.
6. We select 30 minutes 180 degrees.
7. Lists, if we need more, we put another four in the basket.
8. We serve

44.   Potato and onion tortilla in Actifry

Preparation Time: 14 Mins
Serving: 2
Ingredients

- 1 kg of potatoes
- 1 onion
- 8 eggs
- Extra virgin olive oil
- Salt

Preparation

1. Peel the potatoes and cut into flakes.
2. Peel the onion and cut into julienne.
3. We put in the cuvette of the Actifry together with a little salt and a spoonful of extra virgin olive oil.
4. We select 30 minutes.
5. Beat the eggs and dump the potatoes together with the onion. We mix well.
6. We make the tortilla in a large pan, mine 18 cm.
7. We simmer on both sides.
8. We serve

45. Mussels stuffed with tuna in Thermomix

Preparation Time: 30 Mins
Serving: 4

Ingredients

- 1 kg of mussels
- 200 gr of tuna
- 1 onion
- 30 grams of extra virgin olive oil
- 50 gr of wheat flour
- 400 gr of cooking water of mussels
- A little bit of salt
- A little pepper
- A little nutmeg
- Whipped egg and breadcrumbs
- Oil to paint mussels

Preparation

1. Cook the mussels, reserve the broth and remove the meat. We keep the shells.
2. Add the meat to the Thermomix glass and select 5 seconds speed 5. We reserve in a bowl.
3. Now we put the peeled onion and cut into quarters in the Thermomix. We select 5 seconds speed 5.
4. Add the oil and select 5 minutes, temperature varoma, spoon speed.
5. Add the flour and select 3 minutes, temperature varoma, speed 2.
6. Add the mussels cooking broth, mussels meat, drained tuna, salt, ground pepper, nutmeg and select 8 minutes, 100ºC, speed 4.
7. Fill the shells of mussels.
8. We go through beaten egg and breadcrumbs.
9. We place a batch in the bucket of the Airfryer, paint with extra virgin olive oil and select 15 minutes, 180 degrees. We serve

46. Crispy Air-Fried Onion Rings with Comeback Sauce

Preparation Time: 14 Mins
Serving: 2

Ingredients

- 1/2 cup (about a pair of 1/8 oz.) general-purpose flour
- 1 teaspoon preserved paprika
- 1/2 teaspoon kosher salt, divided
- 1 giant egg
- 1 tablespoon water
- 1 cup grain panko (Japanese-style breadcrumbs)
- 1 (10-oz.) sweet onion, dig 1/2-in.-thick rounds and separated into rings
- Cooking spray
- 1/4 cup plain 1 Chronicles low-fat Greek food

- 2 tablespoons canola mayo
- 1 tablespoon tomato ketchup
- 1 teaspoon metropolis mustard
- 1/4 teaspoon garlic powder
- 1/4 teaspoon paprika

Preparations

1. Stir along flour, preserved paprika, and 1/4 teaspoon of the salt in a very shallow dish. Gently beat egg and water in a very second shallow dish. Stir along panko and remaining 1/4 teaspoon salt in a very third shallow dish. Dredge onion rings inside the flour mixture, shaking off excess. Dip in egg mixture, permitting any excess to drip off. Dredge in panko mixture, pressing to stick. Coat each side of onion rings well with preparation spray.

2. Put onion rings in single layer inside air fryer basket, and cook in batches at 375°F till golden brown and tender on each side, 10 minutes, turning onion rings over halfway through preparation. Cowl is stay heat whereas preparation is remaining onion rings.

3. Meanwhile, stir along food, mayonnaise, ketchup, mustard, garlic powder, and paprika in a very tiny bowl till sleek. To serve, place VI to seven onion rings on every plate with a pair of tablespoons sauce.

47.   Air-Fried Corn Dog Bites

Preparation Time: 14 Mins

Serving: 2

Ingredients

- 2 uncured all-beef hot dogs
- 12 craft sticks or bamboo skewers
- 1/2 cup (about a pair of 1/8 oz.) general-purpose flour
- 2 giant eggs, gently crushed
- 1 1/2 cups crushed cornflakes cereal
- Cooking spray
- 8 teaspoons yellow mustard

Preparations

1. Slice every hot dog in lengthwise. Cut every 1 into three equal items. Insert a craft stick or use bamboo skewer into 1 finish of every piece of hot dog.
2. Place flour in a very shallow dish. Place gently crushed eggs in a very second shallow dish. Place crushed cornflakes in a very third shallow dish. Dredge hot dogs inside flour, shaking off excess. Dip in egg, permitting any excess to drip off. Dredge in cornflake crumbs, pressing to stick.
3. Lightly coat air fryer basket is with preparation spray. Place VI corn dog bites in basket; gently spray crack with preparation spray. Cook at 375°F till coating is golden brown and crisp, 10 minutes, turning the corn dog bites over halfway through preparation. Repeat with remaining corn dog bites.
4. To serve, place three corn dog bites on every plate with a pair of teaspoons mustard, and serve instantly.

Nutritional info

- Calories 82
- Fat 3g
- Sat fat 1g
- Unsatfat 1g
- Protein 5g
- Carbohydrate 8g
- Fiber 0g
- Sugars 1g
- Added sugars 0g
- Sodium 179mg
- Potassium 1/3 DV

48.   Air-Fried Apple Chips

Preparation Time: 10 Mins

Serving: 2

Ingredients

- 1 (8-oz.) apple (such as Fuji or Honeycrisp)
- 1 teaspoon ground cinnamon
- 2 teaspoons oil
- Cooking spray
- 1/4 cup plain I Chronicles low-fat Greek food
- 1 tablespoon almond butter
- 1 teaspoon honey

Preparations

1. Thinly slice apple on a mandoline. Place slices in an exceedingly bowl with cinnamon and oil; toss to coat equally.

2. Coat air fryer basket is well with change of state spray. Place seven to eight apple slices in single layer in basket, and cook at 375°F for twelve minutes, turning the slices each four minutes and rearranging slices to flatten them, as they'll move throughout the change of state method. Slices won't be fully crisped, however can still crisp upon cooling. Repeat with remaining apple slices.

3. While apple slices are cook, stir along food, almond butter, and honey in an exceedingly tiny bowl till swish. To serve, place half dozen to eight apple slices on every plate with atiny low small indefinite amount of dipping sauce.

Preparation Time: 20 Mins
Serving: 8
Ingredients

- The egg that we have left over to breach or 1 beaten egg
- Bread crumbs
- Sesame
- Oregano

Preparation

1. We bind the beaten egg with the breadcrumbs until it has dough.
2. We make balls and stretch them into sticks.
3. We go through sesame and oregano that we have linked on a plate.
4. We place in the basket of the Airfryer.
5. We select 20 minutes, 180 degrees.
6. We take out and serve.

Preparation Time: 14 Mins

Serving: 2

Ingredients

- 1 kg mixed minced meat
- 1 onion
- 1 egg
- 1 bunch of parsley
- 2 cloves of garlic
- 1 lemon
- Salt
- Ground pepper
- Bread crumbs
- Extra virgin olive oil

Preparation

1. We put the minced meat inside a bowl.
2. In the Thermomix glass we put the onion cut into quarters, the egg, the parsley, the garlic and the lemon juice.
3. We select 7 seconds speed 5.
4. We dump the content in the minced meat and bind.
5. Add some breadcrumbs so that the meat loses some moisture.
6. We make the meatballs and go through the breadcrumbs.
7. Put the meatballs in batches in the basket of the airfryer and close the drawer.
8. We spray with oil.
9. We select 10 minutes 200 degrees. We shake the basket and leave 3 more minutes.
10. We take out and make another batch of meatballs.
11. So until all are ready. We serve